Two Lenses — Four Europes

Two Lenses — Four Europes

poems & images by

Jim & Carol McCord

Shanti Arts Publishing
Brunswick, Maine

Two Lenses — Four Europes

Copyright © 2019 Jim & Carol McCord

All Rights Reserved
No part of this book may be used or reproduced
in any manner whatsoever without the
written permission of the publisher.

Published by Shanti Arts Publishing
Interior and cover design by Shanti Arts Designs

Shanti Arts LLC
193 Hillside Road
Brunswick, Maine 04011

shantiarts.com

Printed in the United States of America

ISBN: 978-1-947067-63-9 (softcover)
ISBN: 978-1-947067-71-4 (hardcover)

Library of Congress Control Number: 2018963716

*For all dear friends
who have shared their countries,
their homes, their lives with us*

Contents

ENGLAND • North Country Fair and Unfair

In the Beginning	12
Approaching Winter Solstice in York Minster	14
Infant Sorrow	16
Mother and Child in Ripon Cathedral	18
Mount Grace beneath the Hambleton Hills	21
Epiphany Candlemas	23
In the Nave of York St. Mary's	25
Rievaulx Abbey	26
The Foss	28
Late Autumn Fishing in York	30
Seaside Sunday	33
Filey Beach in November	35
Heritage Centre in Whitby	37
Grasmere	38
Briggflatts	41
Yorkshire Dales	44
Lead Mine near Reeth	46
Yorkshire Mines	48
The Iceman Cometh	50
Guy Fawkes in the Vale of York	53
Early Blooming Azalea	55
Monkshood	56
Red Cyclamen	58
My Sunflower	60
Journey	62

FRANCE • Where Light Breathes

Orgues	66
Dolmens	68
Vaunage Stone above Nages	71
In a Church in Villefranche	73
Milton Is Wrong	74
Hermitage	76
Saint-Michel-de-Cuixa	79
Easter Monday	81

ST. VINCENT AMONG THE VINEYARDS	82
PAROISSE PROTESTANTE	84
BUDDHA FOR THICH NHAT HANH	86
SAINT-PAUL DE MAUSOLE	89
BRANCHES OF ALMOND BLOSSOMS	91
A PORTRAIT OF CEZANNE	92
OLIVE TREE	94
MONT SAINTE-VICTOIRE	97
PIGEONNIER	98
WOMAN'S WORK	100
THE WILD BEAST OF COLLIOURE	102
CAZELLE IN WINTER	104
RESURGENCE	107
TEASEL	108
FATHERS AND DAUGHTERS	110
REGGAE VINES	113
VALLEY OF THE TET	114

GREECE • Rock, Clay, Gods

HELLAS	119
ATHENA	121
EARLY ONE MORNING	123
PRIMAL ORIGINS	124
NARCISSUS	127
CYCLADIC POLITICIAN	128
PRIESTESS AT DELPHI	130
DION	132
MOON FLOWERS AT BRAURON	135
TO IRIS	137
THEL IN ZAGORIA	138
VATHIA	141
APOLLO AND DAPHNE	143
CROWN ANEMONE	145
BASSAI	147
KATHARA DEFTERA IN MONEMVASIA	148
MYSTRAS	150
METEORA	152

Two Beasts of Burden	155
Flowering Rock	157
Fishing Early Spring	158
Letter to Yannis Ritsos	160
Mediterranean Cypress	166
Laundry Basket	169
Terraces	170

SPAIN • Andalucía at War and Peace

Christian Light on Moorish Arch	177
Five Centuries	179
British Colonial Pluck	181
Remembrance	183
Two Sides	186
Spanish Dawn	189
Beach Walk	191
The Taste of Earth	192
Cubist Portrait	194
Deeper Than What Is	196
Lorca Returns to Granada	199
Federico Garcia Lorca near Alfacar	201
A Vision	202
Casa de la Alegría	205
Arroyo Hondo	207
Off the Seville-Carmona Road	208
Hidden Remembrance	210
Passage	212
Don Quixote Tilts at Wind Turbines	214
Torre de la Sal	216
Cork Oak	218
Speechless below Benarraba	221
February in Casares	222
No "Thou Shalt Not" in the Valley of Manilva	224
Garden Potpourri at Casa Ceramica	226

Acknowledgments	229
Biographies	231

ENGLAND

North Country Fair and Unfair

In the Beginning

Empty sky, streaked clouds,
swollen hills. Third eye of god
shines on sacred stones.

Approaching Winter Solstice in York Minster

The midday sun still in bed,
barely risen, milky blankets
of sky piled high, its sole eye
catching only tops of pinnacles
and towers. Each measured
limestone block accepts light
according to its aging nature:
warmly, brightly, thankfully,
flatly, rippled, scored, webbed,
fractured, pitted, caverned.

Inside, Advent darkness waits
for candlelight. The procession
spreads solemnly from west to east,
from door to altar. Candles flare,
sputter, catch, sputter out,
refuse to light, like the face of
the sub-chanter leading children
back to the west door. At the hem
of his robe a girl of five, her
eyes shining with tears of fright.

I feel no joy or glory here.
How cold the cold. How far beyond
ceremony and fear lies light?
How deeply set in stone? How dark
must darkness be? How black your
night? Why blind to sight? Why
deaf to hear? At this moment
I want only that lazy white
sun outside to toss and turn
with, make radiant love with.

Infant Sorrow

I can see you,
abandoned child,
though your sculptor
perched you high
on a cliff face
like a hungry eaglet
crying out for food.

I hear your howl,
feel the loss you feel
but cannot understand,
sicken to see your human
body begin to match
your mind made savage
by beastly suffering.

Mother and Child in Ripon Cathedral

— for Paul

Herod's decree whips Mary with its
nine knotted tails. Her body tightens
like a welded seam. Her throat a crevasse
with walls of flesh in 18 gauge copper sheets,
a cancer window left unframed by a careless
surgeon. The infant's skull a fractured
globe of overlapping plates. No burnished
words. Touches only of polish on shrapnel
and in the gesture toward silent melodies.

Mary rapt with eyes half-closed feeds
the child on notes that sway from joy
to sorrow, hope to despair. Her vision
of what's to be presses like a nail into flesh.
The babe in swaddling hands looks skyward,
hollow eyes blank to human sacrifice.

From Lent to Easter in this market town
all public icons wear sack cloth for symbol's sake.

Mount Grace beneath the Hambleton Hills

Restored to grid-outline ruins,
the priory is again a walled garden
surrounded by woodland wilderness,
the remains of its church cradled
in the arms of grassy cloisters.
Twelve young trees brace in autumn,
endure winter, leaf and stretch
in spring and summer. On loan
in the roofless choir stands
The Madonna of the Cross, its
maker's stylized Mary with child
held breast high in transom arms
to combine Nativity, Resurrection,
Crucifixion, Ascension.

I see the intent but feel trapped
by a text heady as the New Testament
and physical as the polystyrene
and fiberglass polished with wax
that shape the sculptor's statement.
A pallet knife textures molded
details on the two figures.
Scalpel, please, to rid all minds
of doctrine and open hearts with
grace. Like corrective surgery on
a tree that's been wrongly strapped,
or on a young man and woman coming
of age caged like lion and lamb
in what they are told is paradise.

Epiphany Candlemas

There was more light tonight
than at Advent, more human
movement in and out of nave,
along aisles, up and down
pulpit stairs, behind altars.
But the words still rang dull
as untried gold which no
myrrh could heal. Thank god
for the organ and choir
rising like frankincense
past decorated piers to
simpler arches and beyond.

In the Nave of York St. Mary's

—for Annette

Blind springs search for light
they nourish but never see.
Flames flicker in glass
cups, prick watery memory,
stir souls housed in stone to speech.

Rievaulx Abbey

— for Harry and Ginit

Nest of stone tucked in
wooded bank. High altar now
bird bath for rock doves.

The Foss

— for George

York's other river
like a second son
or daughter. Beloved
in hushes, free
of great expectations,
happy to be unnoticed,
content to flow
at its own pace,
pleased to receive
reflections of stone
and brick on its slender
body. A sibling with
character compared
to first-born boastful
Ouse with ancient towers,
grand bridges, parks,
pubs, tourist boats.

Late Autumn Fishing in York

— for BK

On Saturdays fishermen beat the sun
to the block-stone, cement-embanked Foss.
Ribbons from reflected street lamps swim
like trout in the river. Car boots emptied,
rods connected, lines baited. Propped
poles nod with sleepy heads that rise
and fall with flood-controlled waters.
Umbrellas protect from spitting rain.
The men smoke, chat, squint toward fish
too small and deep to see. They do not
notice each round stone precisely set
in the cobbled walk, have no interest
in Izaak Walton angling with fly and cork
on pastoral banks in revolutionary times.
Yet, like Walton, their finest catches
are friendship, live speech. Behind them,
a pensioner in Kirkholm plaid with precise
flip of the wrist casts bits of bread
to honking, waddling, undignified geese.

Seaside Sunday

Gulls cry for attention
against the sound of spent waves
at Canary Ledges. Everything moves
toward its own dissolve: ocean swells
exhale in the broad cove, crests
bubble and pop, breakers slide
to rocky shore, trees hang on
for life in the pocked cliff face
of Black Ven. A woman mends
her child's swimsuit beneath a yellow
umbrella. On gray sands a man splits
rocks to find fossils. Ammonites
lie still, sea-changed into spinning
spines and ribbings rich and strange.

Filey Beach in November

— for Lesley and Roger

Under a sun wrapped
in shroud and a brig
dull as a winter plover
the photographer
alone, flockless,
squints for flecks
of light to see
more than gray
until like a wild-eyed
turnstone flicking
pebbles in search
of food she catches
shadows playing
with shades truer
than sunlight and pipes
like an oystercatcher.

Heritage Centre in Whitby

180 million years ago Monkey
Puzzle trees bathed in shallow
seas and warm swamps, settled
in sand and mud, became fissile
crystals: jet. Black for Albert's
mourning Queen matched her coal-
crusted midland cities, flowing dress
and crape band, her pain veined deep
as uncut stone in Whitby's cliff.

Today Alec MacKenzie sculpts
pendants and pins from the 85 lb.
block of jet he found one lucky
morn. Treadle wheels rough cut,
powders hone, chamois polish.
He gifted us one virgin piece
with swirling wood rings furrowed
by worm tracks preserved like
prehistoric trenches in a tar pit.

He also crafted for my wife a pair
of pitch black earrings with ammonite
eyes, they the shape of teardrops
once shed only in private quarters.

Grasmere

—for Maggie

Wordsworth's Hobbit cot sits embedded
in hillside, innards dark as a coffin.
Pub beams like a lid over flagstone
black as coal, the silent, hidden spring
beneath. Elsewhere: empty pantries,
a canopied four-poster shrouded in heavy
curtains, newspapers for wallpaper hung
to fight cold. Its outer dress in modest
protest: white-washed walls cover pebble
dash and a mad mix of local stone placed
by hand in dry horizontal bands chiseled
to edge windows, doors, cornerstones.

In this tiny goldcrest nest, William's
women kept watch for supper orders, scribal
tasks, peat fires paling to glow. He wrote
upstairs in filtered light, windows pocked
like the face of Grasmere Lake when rain
fell like cherry stones. Outdoors on slippery
paths he counted syllables with each step,
lost himself in his own measured music
of sweetly sorrowful nightingale notes.

Today Corpse Road still runs past Dove's
door from Ambleside, the same Coffin
Stone snug against the bank where bearers
once rested their heavy load on the muddied
route to holy Oswald's consecrated ground.
Beneath a dark, dense yew in the churchyard
the poet's family plot fences bodies long
gone to bone, free of earth's diurnal course.
William's simple headstone sinks slightly
left, as if unsure of the sureness of faith,
as if in doubt with overhanging yew
this world could ever bathe itself in light.

BRIGGFLATTS

—for Joseph

No crackling Fox fire hereabout,
no furnace blast out of mouth,
the preacher's rock pulpit
four miles up the road dumb

for three hundred fifty years.
Now maggots feast while bees
comb blossoms, wheat fields
and fells meet bracken moors.

No music to maul either,
no tenor bull in field.
Notes dissolve in clouds,
words sink in riverbank.

An overcoat of stone protects
plank, panel, and turned oak
in the Quaker meeting house
where pulses beat beyond speech.

– continued

Every birth a silent hope,
every life a silent trial.
Neighbors warm to God,
ice with fear of slowworm.

Fifty meters up a single track
road the burial ground slopes
north and east. Closest to its
gate, Basil Bunting's headstone

welcomes afternoon shade. Enough
of day. His chiseled name with
dates of birth and death fade.
Commonplace grass covers plot.

No need for swingers of axe
or strong song. No need to force
love or battle loveless nights.
No need for star guide. Silence.

Overhead a single beech buds
leaves that drift to ground. Now.

Yorkshire Dales

— for Eric

are my kind of poetry, an ancient landscape
worked and reworked with keen eye and mind
by farming generations for living's sake.
Only the ridges — rough coats of moorland
bracken flecked with heather — are free
from human touch. Upland fields spread
shaggy as their sheep, midland fields
gentle as pampered cattle. Woodlands swell,
stone walls flow down to rivers that twist
like thick jungle vines or sweet pea coils.

Despite the rub through centuries, there's
grace between man and land, animal and rock,
present and past. At Conistone gray wall set
stone by stone gives more light than gray
sky. Blackbirds hardy as flint in Littondale
nest in rotted post holes of derelict barns.
In Dentdale a gray heron drifts above late
summer shallows, glides beneath a pack
horse bridge, lands soft as down on sandy
banks cleared with care by farmer's hands.

Lead Mine near Reeth

"Welcome," greets the director
of human resources at hell-mouth.
"Watch your head and quiet, please.
Satan's asleep, but his wings
can split rock when he stirs.
Dante's pure ore compared to us.
No augured guilt here at Grinton,
no sins to punish. We work bodies,
leave souls to shift as they can.

That your lad? He'll do well to haul
out bucketed bouse and deads.
Water, too, if shaft sides soften.
He'll grow your hardy shoulder fellow.
Shilling a day for him, 2/8 for you.
How about your wife? Any daughters?
We need family crews and you need
crowdy of oatmeal, potatoes, suet,
bread with a light smear of butter.

Company has picks, hammers, feathers
for hire. By the week, plus wear and
tear. We also do candles and powder.
You can work thirty years if you're not
crushed up before. Keep an eye out
for kicking horses, rolling trolleys.
Cuts and bruises are part of cramped
innards. With ventilation shafts,
no worry at Grinton of choke damp.

Less lead poisoning here than at Old Gang.
Arthritis about average, consumption
worse in London. Palsy and spluttering
of black spit common fare everywhere.
Despair fairly rare. And after six days
picking veins, there's sunlight and heather
when the season's right, a white-washed
church in the village with hope for a place
nowhere to be found inside this hill."

Yorkshire Mines

Miners with iron hammers in these cushion hills
worked days black as night to desecrate earth's body.
Land flayed for two thousand years: furnace holes
incised between valley ribs, needle shafts drilled
to drain heart's core, ore drawn through veins, lead
stripped for dressing, woodlands bared for smelting.

Peat stores now empty as stopes, chimneys like crematoria.

At Ribbledale on the viaduct anchored in the pebbled river bed
of Batty Moss a tourist train steams past sacred Pen-Y-Ghent.

The Iceman Cometh

When cold is so cold you can't
feel the coldness of it —

when your fingers are like
limbs of a tree sheathed in ice —

you have to go a long way away —

as far as a satellite without
its own light like the moon —

to take even a nibble of warmth
and leave behind echoes of your breath.

Guy Fawkes in the Vale of York

November night cuts like a splinter
of ice sharp as winter moonlight.

Seasoned twigs, sticks, branches
feed the purging blaze, feast

on scarecrow Fawkes. Flannel, denim,
straw ignite red, blue, white.

Fiery tongues atop the teepee
hip-hop like lusty boys and girls,

spit fire flies and ember stars
at the mouth of the hungry moon.

Hell-bent coals beneath settle in,
lose aura, accept their ashen glow.

Early Blooming Azalea

— planted for Lillian

It's cliché we die like flowers,
hard to accept that's all there is.
Some favor stone in unkempt graveyards,
some ashes spread on calming seas.

Reincarnation's fancy fiction,
rebirth vain hope not worth belief.
I deny thoughts of after places,
try to greet death as life's due ease.

So I work hard to have this flower
fill empty spaces outside and in.
Planted in shade close by my window,
it feeds a need to see earth live.

In early spring come flared azaleas,
orange buds tucked in yellow flames.
Still grazed by all that brings a darkness,
this is one light my eye can hold.

Monkshood

Your galea like a cowl, Englishmen
call you monkshood. But you're
also known as devil's helmet
and you wear your two selves
well — cure like a monk, poison
like a fiend, ease arthritis
and slow a too-fast heart,
tip arrows for instant kills
and make werewolves of women.
Either way, your dark, velvet beauty
signals the end of rainbow summer.

Red Cyclamen

When autumn freezes russet mums
and winds chill blocks of brick
you appear a pendant conch
capped with comical sepal hat.

You stay ten days a stunted self
until the time your calyx splits,
unwinds five tongues of twisting
flame soft as a baby's skin.

With stem well-settled into corm,
petals lean toward frosted panes
exchanging words ember-warm
till speech and body fade.

Then petals darken at each tip
and blood retreats through slackened
veins to look just like my father's
looked and like my mother's after him.

You show me life for what it is
this silent, meditative night.
I thank you for your candidness
for stirring thoughts of clear, hard light.

My Sunflower

— to William Blake

Ah, Sunflower! defiant of time
Caring not for the steps of the Sun
Nor seeking its sweet golden clime
Knowing here all journeys are done.

Where the Youth can fulfill his desire
And his Lover her beauty can show
My Sunflower needs not aspire
Beyond radiant earth to go.

Journey

Take me on your boat, oarsman,
past black banks, lead hills,
lake of spectral woe —
beyond watery reflection
to the dawn of mindful light.

FRANCE

Where Light Breathes

Orgues

Organs outdoors
play to sky
and brambles,
sigh and howl
with the wind,
lose pieces
of themselves
in hard rain,
soft showers,
till bellows slow,
pipes struggle
for air, notes
fade, keyboards
dissolve to grains
of sand. Above
cathedral walls
choirs of skylarks
in soprano-trill
soar dawn to dusk.

Dolmens

Perhaps a portal tomb,
perhaps no grave at all,
simply a stone table
with unfinished edges
that scraped the knees
of giants when they dined.

Some face east, some
backside solstice suns.
Some shrouded in earth,
some open to sky. Axes
and gold in a few, flow
of air only in others.

Today a farmer's
shelter or henhouse.

Vaunage Stone above Nages

When my eye deadens this so-called "lush,
hilly country with slumberous villages," I see
only brown plains of stubble on a forgotten
seabed, vineyard heads with barbed wire hair,
and bourgeois villages set into the sides
of knolls spotted with scrub oak, stunted pine,
fruitless olive. I know then it's time to climb
the rocky path up snow-clad Les Castels.

I count my steps on flat white stones
as centuries reclaimed. At the oppidum
imagined men fix spear heads and sharpen
knives for me. Old women with pestles grind
grain old men store in fired pots. Young
women pluck eyebrows, dab perfume from
colored vials. Wives jingle bracelets
of bright glass. Boys and girls squeal.

On my descent life stirs in the pure waters
of our Roman spring and in pale green fields,
in seeing school children midday harnessed
to bulging backpacks that make them wobble,
in watching old men stoop at *pétanque*
under rows of leopard-spotted Plane trees.
In the fragrance of almond blossoms
I know I'll smell in three weeks or four.

In a Church in Villefranche

—for Jo

This man braided in body and mind
couldn't be suffering the burden of humanity
suffering. The reason has to be closer, less
abstract. You can tell from the way his flesh
has left him he's been flayed to bone
with the hope we could see more clearly
his heart still beat, his lungs still fill.

He must be feeling a pain more tortuous
than godly pain. If psychologists have it right,
he's lost not a mother, father, wife, or lover,
but son or daughter. A son like the one off
to war receiving a last kiss from his mother
on the memorial down the street. Or a maiden
daughter as gentle and selfless as Ruth
when she gleaned corn in a land she did not
know and winnowed it on the threshing floor.

If you accept this, the 'O' which is his mouth
is not a plea seeking forgiveness for others.
It's either a silent scream louder than pain
can voice or the howl of one turned beast.

Milton Is Wrong

— for Hugh

"I cannot praise a fugitive and cloistered virtue,
unexercised and unbreathed . . .
that which purifies us is trial."
— John Milton, *Areopagitica*

Praise be to cloistered virtue
where the world is pictured whole,
dust and heat, ash and breath
with every contemplative step.
St. Benedict's rule to pray and work
taken simple as a monk's cell makes
lean the monk who follows it. Gallery
exercise east to west, north to south,
fires thought until full truth glows
like unforgotten embers.

At best a central garden free of thorns
is half the story, at worst desperate
fiction to hang vain hope upon. Marble
capitals tell it all: birth and joy,
trial and death, human adoration and
abhorrence. Griffon guards, smug serpents,
kings and shepherds, court jester, Sumo
wrestler clutched with dragon, lewd monkey
at the feet of seraph, pelicans kissing.
Revelation chiseled, sculpted, crafted.

Hermitage

To get to this ancient chapel
on the flank of Catalones
you need the eye of a raptor,
the sure-footedness of a goat
that knows the uneven way,
the determination of a boar
hounded by bay dogs.

Tracks of dirt and rubble
wind through thickets
of oak and juniper, shrubs
of knee-high tree heather,
rosemary, wild thyme. Branches
prick like butterfly needles,
smell of chaparral lifts spirits.

A trek to see what a life
of solitude, silence, prayer
and stone for penance left behind.
Garden now a desert. Fallen
rocks like chips from dry bone.
Empty bell tower with both eyes
to the sky. Door always locked.

Saint-Michel-de-Cuixa

> *"Oh! Blessed rage for order, pale Ramon . . ."*
> — Wallace Stevens,
>   "The Idea of Order at Key West"

After the revolution slumlords
turned this church into a Luftwaffe
ruin. Innards filled with oak beams,
roof tiles, wall rock. Crypt the home
for asp vipers, cells webbed by spiders,
cloister overrun with thorns, thistles,
briers, water fouled. Sounds only
of breeze sighing through post holes,
wind threading its way through brambles.

Today order is restored. Buildings
sealed tight as the rules for communal
life, robes mended, psalms intoned.
The majestic tower rises to stretch
toward heaven along with the wispy poplar
beside it and arrows of cypress nearby.
Outside the compound grapevines pruned,
pinched, trellised, and spaced equally
in rows straight as the closure wall.

All bounded by God's golden compasses.
Majestic Mount Canigou chills at the sight.

Easter Monday

Two old women
shuffle through
chilly morn
to sing Catalan
sorrows and joys.
Bodies bowed in pain
and reverence, each
step on the uneven
path a challenge met.
Between cap on head
and espadrilles on feet
black shawls mourn,
red dresses celebrate.
In the village square
a choir of friends
helps to warm stones
in winter walls,
welcomes green shoots
on vines that climb
in unpredictable webs
like history.

St. Vincent among the Vineyards

— for Howard

Such a blank expression, Vincent,
no sign of faith unshakeable, no clue
that angels visited or heavenly light
flooded your cell. Your portrait incised
on this Romanesque archway tells nothing
of your steeled devotion or of joints
cracked on the rack, flesh furrowed
with iron hooks, gashes salted for flavor
before fired on gridiron and cooled
like a smithy's slack tub in the sea.

I suspect no vintner chose to believe
either legend, needed to bring you
down to earth, needed a saint to adopt
for healthy vines, good fortune. Vincent
"Vin-sang" then transformed, his bloody
wine to flow like sap from pruned winter
vines. Between dormancy and bud-break,
limbs clipped to stubs, shoots sheered.
On his holy day: blessings and bonfires,
feasts and dance, music and drunkenness.

Paroisse Protestante

We dress in our Sunday best
to attend service in a temple
800 years old built of block
stone solid as the killing
faith of Templars. Its tower
bell hangs in a simple metal
frame. Inside, upper apse
and ceiling plaster-troweled
smooth as local cotton. No icon
or saint dares show its face
in this home of Huguenots.
Between the modern keyboard
and podium, a young woman in
olive trousers and green fatigue
jacket ushers us through songs,
readings, brief prayers, a sermon.
Deaf to meaning, we're stunned
dumb by the poetry: a concert
of measured lines, cadences,
accents, pauses, human voice.

No music of the spheres
or prosaic priest allowed
in this temple of Nages.

Buddha for Thich Nhat Hanh

Legs heavy as earth,
Arms and fingers light as air,
Mind at peace with both.

Saint-Paul de Mausole

Van Gogh's first view of the asylum
through olive orchards was of walls
thick and tall as ramparts. Inside,
basket-handle corridors arched over him,
offered protection as a refuge should.

In his room one metal bed with thin
mattress, one worn chair, two sea-
green curtains. With shutters open
to the sun, bottles on the windowsill
turned from black to indigo, wavy
panes softened the edges of iron
bars and undulated the garden below.

Four attacks followed: anxieties
to terrorize, nightmares to torment.
"Inner seizures of despair," he called
them. After each, his eye refocused mind
toward light, forced him and easel out
into it — past box trees and fenced
fields to quarries and chasms beneath
the Apilles whose sides flowed for him
like lava above foothills of sea swells.

Branches of Almond Blossoms

Van Gogh gave his namesake nephew
the only gift he could afford —
a double portrait. Spots of white
uncurl from buds as if birthing.
Clusters of star blossoms on sunlit
branches celebrate their coming. Silk
petals spin from unruly boughs twisted
in crazy directions. The subject, he
wrote, after a third seizure, slowed
him down, calmed his fevered mind
until his brush regained its touch.

He would see his brother's son only
in cradle, never know how severe the boy's
illness or how pained his life without
a father. So no cry of anguished paint,
buds, blossoms, and branches together
backed by soothing sky-blue. In noisy
Paris, his silent gift hung above
the family piano as sane accompaniment
for just six weeks until Theo —
brother, husband, father, provider —
fell crazed beyond sight with syphilis.

A Portrait of Cezanne

Cezanne said sensitivity
defines the individual
but he won't let me near him.
I'd like him to offer me
a handshake so I could feel
how strong or not his grip.
I'd like to look him in the
eye, in both eyes that see
so much. I'd like to touch
his paint-smeared smock,
take away as tokens bits
of an emerald tree, Prussian
blue lake, clump of earth
as orange as roofs of sunlit
houses in L'Estaque. I'd like
to hear his country accent,
hear how witty and ironic
he really is, or isn't. I want
him to be more than painting.
But he hides from me behind
decorative screens and in folds
of tablecloths. He blends
with the surface of a glazed
ginger jar or melancholy
old apple. He fades behind
brocade curtains of words
such as cone, sphere, cylinder.
When he doesn't disappear
I see him as one of his skulls
on an Oriental rug, his eye
sockets giving off a bluish
thought for me to flesh out.

Olive Tree

— for Carol

This olive tree is not on Cezanne's terrace.
It is not the one he protected from builders
who threw stone, wood, and plaster cast-offs
thoughtlessly into his garden. It's not
the tree he talked to, listened to, sometimes
kissed that grew in strength from the attention.
Not the one that knew his life story or the one
he desired to be buried beneath. This is not
the piece of nature he left a living being,
chose not to express in paint with geometric eye.

What you see is an untouched photograph
of an olive tree. It's an object in Provence
alive with sensation because respected, then
loved, by its viewer. A tree free of theories
about intersecting planes, textures, surface
and depth, vibrations of light, tone, color.
It stands like a wise elder who sees more
than the plowed field before her and spring
brush behind. In each of her arms a galaxy
of silver stars whitens our night sky.

Mont Sainte-Victoire

> *"One minute of the world goes by. To paint it in its reality! And to forget everything for that. To become the minute itself."*
> — Paul Cezanne

To look at this mountain and never see it
the same way is to see it as it is
and paint it as it isn't. If it had a tongue
it might tell us just how sharp its peak,
how graceful its back, how thick or sparse
its maquis and holm oak jacket. It might even
explain its name and let us know if its chasm
heals with grass meadows pure as heaven or
poisons with the blood of Teutons vile as hell.

The sun shifts its gaze on it every second,
slides along its faces, noses into hollows,
lips ledges until stopped by shadow, seeks
shelter behind clouds as filaments of rays,
hides completely behind gray. Under its
watch the mountain can turn moonstone
to black in the blink of an eye. Under the
painter's eye it becomes a volcano stilled
by planes that tilt, divide, and interlock.

Cezanne picks the view and time of day,
makes his way under clear skies by foot
or carriage to paint, he says, "its reality."
His brush dabs canvas like shutter clicks
of a camera. He has no interest in illuminate
light, snatches colors it reflects to catch
moments he must know can never be caught.
While he labors the mountain struggles
to free itself from legend, history, him.

Pigeonnier

This cylinder with dunce cap
was designed for a noble game
played by aristocrats. A heated
sport not for the pigeon-hearted
or -livered. Pigeons housed
in luxury flats. A pigeon standard
for show of power and wealth
to generate more plucked flesh
than anyone could eat, more eggs
than anyone could suck, more
dung than anyone could plow
into sterile earth. The shit so hot
it scorched seeds impotent on the spot.

Woman's Work

A red and black speck
distant as lifetimes
makes her way with mop
and plastic bucket
in one hand, straw bag
in other, on legs
like medieval columns
among cobbled houses
and under archways
of cut and rough stone
ancient as her task.

The Wild Beast of Collioure

— for Bruce

I often wonder if Matisse chose
this town that summer for beach,
chateau, Notre Dame des Anges,
or the commune's famed anchovies.
I like to think it was the last.

He foraged the port like one
of the slippery, filter-feeding
creatures, splashed his palette
with oily colors, painted boats
and sea raw as a raw aphrodisiac
with strong, pungent flavor.
He gutted objects of shadow
and line, salted and pickled
them to preserve their wildness.

Critics choked as if poisoned
by domoic acid from the gut
of the small fish. Matisse downed
pizza topped with anchovies fresh
from tins of vinegar marinade.

Cazelle in Winter

Igloo of stone,
micro-geodesic dome,
Himalayan tent
staked against cold
winds to shelter sheep
and warm farmhands
who peek through eye
slits at scrub oak
woods to clear, fence
posts to wire, gray
fields to sow green.

Resurgence

Restless fountains burst
from mouths of cleft limestone.
Crystals drip from sleeping bats
to quench the thirst of spring,
heal fields and farms.

Teasel

— for Chris

It would be a pity if you
were only a piece of a poem —
prickly as a teasel stem, or
an egg with porcupine quills,
or a teasel leaf like drapery
in a Renaissance painting,
or a weedy head with the arms
of ballerinas arched over it.

I think you deserve more, Old World
herb, growing wild beside our country
roads. Before wire teeth there
were your hooked bracts to raise
nap, card, tease, and clean wool
until each hairy strand combed
in precise line with each other
lay readied for spinning wheels.

Fathers and Daughters

— for Shawne

Rows of poplars in early
spring draw for me sweet
thoughts from winter wells.
They're not muscular
as wrestlers like Plane
trees lining the road
they scurry from, or
precious as debutantes
like pink peach blossoms
nearby. They're tall,
straight-backed, slender
as girly teens dressed
in feathered branches
with modest crests.
They speak in whispers,
quiver in breezes.
Wispy beauties planted
by fathers to attract
husbands. An investment
from babyhood, a dowry
rich as rooted love.

[N.B. When a girl is born in some parts of Calabria her father plants a row of poplar trees for her. By the time she is seventeen the poplars are large, fine, and ready to be hewn down. Their wood is then sold and the money set aside for the daughter's dowry.]

Reggae Vines

Dreadlocks of Shiva
braided amidst wildflowers
dance the king's music.

Valley of the Tet

— for Michael and Richard

Sunrise rich as rose garnet.

Snow-topped Canigou to see.

Mourning doves to hear.

Rosemary to smell.

Clementines to taste.

Warm air to touch.

Sunset rich as rose garnet.

No need to dream.

[N.B. Garnet is a legendary gemstone in the Catalan region. In ancient times it was thought to have many virtues because it symbolized loyalty and truth, and protected from diabolical influences and dangers.]

GREECE
Rock, Clay, Gods

Hellas

Daystar bleaches
all hope of rain,
seas gutted of fish,
cities choke on exhaust
and marble dust, horns
and sirens wheeze.

Rock mountains
hard as lost pride.

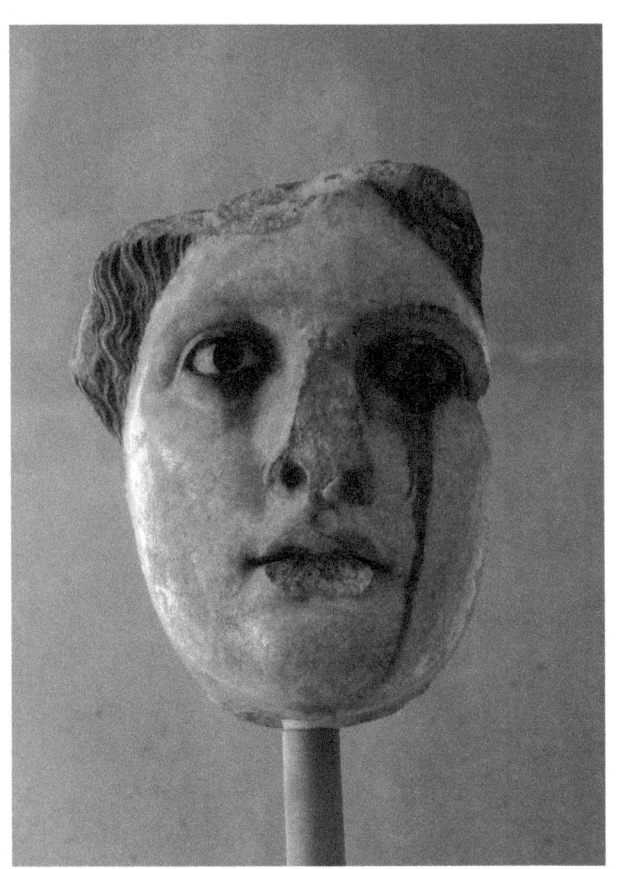

Athena

Where lies wisdom,
gray-eyed goddess?

In the power of war
or power of peace?

In the bloodied field
or olive tree?

In the flashing sword
or craftsman's shop?

Early One Morning

Athena Nike has gone to pot says
the sculptor of the bulky, unburnished
bronze in Kolonaki Square. She's a hippo
goddess in a one-piece stretch dress,
her legs open so you can catch a glimpse
of her privates. Only the stringless
lute on her fat lap is polished smooth.

Headlessly she sprawls, legs pocked
like her breasts, back slit open like
a slaughter house pig's to show off
her twisted spine. Her single sign of past
victories is one wing growing askew
from the left blade of her upper back.
There's no doubt Nike has gone to pot.

I leave her for the central fountain in
the Square and look askance to see a lean,
old hag across from me. She trembles from
the cold and trembling fidgets to find
the pastry in the tissue envelope she holds.
But she shakes too much, and her mumbled
street Greek cannot unfold the mystery.

Her face and hands and legs shine midnight
blue blotched here and there with blackest
red. She looks. She fingers. She fiddles.
She cries out to draw from me, perhaps,
the thought that beneath her woolen shawl
of black curves a steely back to support
two empowered wings of aery, feathered gold.

Primal Origins

The Parian marbles from the Temple
of Zeus at Olympia speak severely
of how we shake beasts out to become
Gods, shake Gods out and become beasts.

The central figures distant, iced.
Exquisite Apollo in the west oversees
with vacant eyes the rape of Lapiths
come to the wedding of Pirithous.
Relaxed Zeus in the east feels
the guile of Pelops beside him,
knows Oinomaus' cruel game is up.
Confidence of godly justice to feed
itself forever on human irony, get
strong on the blood of human failure.

The only troubled spectators an old seer
or philosopher — perhaps just old man —
and two women on their bellies fear-struck
in disbelief under the pressing roof
of the northwest pediment. Each smells
the stench of mortality in the breath
of drunken centaurs, in the torn flesh
and dung they'll leave on the palace floor.

Only Deidamia blessed with Apollonian
understanding stands above indignities. She
stares blank-eyed as if feeling not at all
the centaur's left hand pressing its wet palm
to her breast, his right inching toward groin,
her thigh locked by his hoof. In heroic mask
she freezes against the lust filled man-horse.

When she becomes immortal stone, the gods rejoice.
When Theseus drives the centaurs from the hall,
the gods rejoice again. Later, Pirithous —
hot for Kore — has his heels cooled in Hades.

Narcissus

You're a proud boy to scorn
all love from others, naive
to think you'll grow old
as an oak that way. It's
unnatural at twenty with
seismic shocks of desire
to reject the stalking body
of a wood nymph in full bloom.

You leave yourself nowhere
to go for love except to self.

So you bathe in your father's
river to feel your marbled flesh.
Your mother's waters rush
over you, turn marble into
sensual throbbing. You yearn
for a flirtatious image
in a fountain clear as silver,
drown of thirst for yourself.

A flower now trumpets your
folly for us to hear, its
plaints of unfilled love echo,
echo over your white and gold
head of narcotic fragrance.

Cycladic Politician

Eyeless, earless, mouth-less
for keen senses of smell and touch.
Wafer-thin forehead where a brain normally lodges.
Thick neck from years of playing rock ball.
Arms crossed in feigned submission.
Marble hard, dense, impenetrable.

Priestess at Delphi

The charioteer in the museum
looks stoned but never flew
so high as the exemplary peasant
woman seated on a tripod perched
over a fracture in the ground,
both ears cocked to hear Apollo's
pronouncements while inhaling
earthy gases till her eyes glazed,
heart raced, body convulsed
and speech erupted in tongues
for priests to interpret in words
coherent, poetic, politic, ambiguous.

The original huffer civilized.

Dion

— for Flora and her daughters

It's best to visit this sacred
site of Zeus before Easter,
before orthodox Priests intone Odes
of Lamentation, incense dizzies,
vigil candle spreads its light
to faithful disciples. Before
the resurrection of a man
fills the faithful with fire.

Wander the grounds like Demeter
in search of her lost daughter.
Leave all thoughts of mankind
behind. No need to identify
the women: Hera or handmaid,
Isis or devotee, Artemis. All
stand quiet watch over sanctuary,
temple springs, lake, trees, rock.

All grace banks of reeds, paths
of weed, pillars of marble,
stone reliefs from broken altars.
Look until you find one walking
into being from a spring once
the dwelling place of the Muses.
Listen to her sing as she rises
from embryonic waters.

Moon Flowers at Brauron

This marshland outpost free from Athenian
machismo survived the flooding waters
of Erasinos and threat of female memory lost.

Artemis came first with bow, crescent
moon, girls. A sacred spring rose to wash
foul civilization from her body
strong and hard as temple stone.

Iphigenia followed with a wooden statue
of the impassioned goddess in cart, set
her upright on an island of bedrock
and spent her life holding tight
the sanctuary keys to receive with tears
garments of joy from new mothers, garments
of sorrow from mothers cradling stillborns.

Her flower-headed maidens stretched necks
slender as stems to rival Apollo's sun,
welcomed puberty by dancing as saffron
baby bears to the confusion of boys.
Like twilight in late spring, virgins
set stoa and courtyard aglow before
they left for Argos, Athens, husbands.

Today a cool breeze links swampy
refuge with the broad valley beyond.
From the ridge between I spot sun-bathed
crown daisies beside dark euphorbia,
chrome yellow blossoms scraping
their cheeks against the shrub's lace
of protective thorns.

To Iris

Show off your flashy sepal dress
as if it were made of petals. Catch
a breeze, wave your white cuffs
to summer sun and cloudless sky,
your purple sleeves to passing day.

If ancient gods still lived
you'd be earth's messenger to remind
them of earthly beauties fragile
as a rainbow nourished by particles
of mist in a momentary spray of light.

Thel in Zagoria

On the cobbled path to Ayia Panaskevi
I saw Thel lead a small, shorn flock,
her arms sinewy as rigging, her body
tap-rooted deep as an olive tree.

She'd discarded flowing gown
for black woolen shirt and cap,
her shepherdess' crook
for twisted walking stick.

Blake's dark dawn had given way
to acceptance of dusk. I imagined
her womb empty as a cell in an empty
monastery, her mind faintly lit

like the thin candle left by passersby
who stop to ask forgiveness. She filled
the chill air around with gentle talk
to her sheep, kept the bleating band

together in relaxed line. Each wood-
collared bell rang a singular note
that echoed down Vikos Gorge past
thickets of holly oak to rock beds below.

When I passed, Thel greeted me twice: first
with eyes of evening light free of agonizing
memory, second with a toothless smile
broad and comforting as her vales of Har.

Vathia

Half alive in present, half dead
in past. Close living and bloody
feuds. Fortress towers now
gutted walls. One chair, one
metal cot in an abandoned hovel.
Hilltop views of sea and bay.
Hillside smothered in wildflowers.

In the frame of one doorway
I catch the eye of a survivor
in black dress, black hood,
and wonder her thoughts when
she sees with her deep-set
eyes the sun set each night
and rise each morning.

Apollo and Daphne

Whenever I pass a laurel tree
I see Daphne's outstretched
arms, her fingers turn to sprigs,
her thighs to bark for woody
immortality. And I see the god
of plague in heat like a rabid
buck, hear his song screech
like a randy cock, and his lyre
grate like the caw of his ravens.

Prophecy suspended for lust.
Eyes slave to loins, hands
to the touch of the nymph's flesh.
Her scent and his imagined taste
of violation drown her howls.
It's not possible for me then
to smell the aromatic leaves
or delicate spring flowers
of this mortal, sweet bay tree.

Crown Anemone

Adonis is no god
but his flower glows
immortal on its
capillary stem
with black stigma
where the boar's
tusk sank into
his youthful loins.

Revived by Venus
with nectar sweet
as honey, fragrant
as oil of jasmine,
he became the wind's
fragile son, a whorl
of flesh inside
bleeding corolla.

He blooms in open
meadows and grasslands,
his petals silk fans
doomed to be scattered
by breezes. He's a button
of blood to remind us
of a lost love as pure
as his lover's white swans.

Bassai

In rock mountains uninhabited
by man or centaur this pentad
of conservation tents bleached
white as the sun houses a thank you

temple to Apollo-healer for sending
plague its foul way. P. T. Barnum
could not have squeezed his show
into it. No room for high wire

acts and no rings to master.
Nor could Calder have carved
its Corinthian capital, though
his circus to delight moon-eyed

children with mouths open wide
as Arcadian skies would fit easily
between its fluted columns now banded
like anklets on prancing elephants.

Outside, acrobats hand walk on rock
walls, vault over anchored cables,
tumble through scrub brush with tears
in their eyes. I've been told

they're rehearsing for the day
the temple casts its wrapping aside.
The day its pillars will shine
like spears of victory to the sky.

Kathara Deftera in Monemvasia

To cleanse the body and set
sin aside one Monday a year
is small sacrifice. To heal
wounds five hundred years old
festering, weeping, not so.

If only for today Venetian
musicians play in our square
for solemn Byzantine priests.
West at peace with East,
carnival with crucifixion.

Mystras

It's worth the change to be
a donkey for the day and hoof
your way on steps and stones
jagged as the mountain ridges
above, serpentine as the valley
roads below. View churches
with walls of hieroglyphs,
domes like balloons, fresco
saints with aureoles, arms
heads, feet, robes dissolving
into stone on their way toward
immortality. A mother with baby
on lap softens you up before
the hard truths of doubt, betrayal,
denial, judgment, torture, death.

The larger the church, the viewer
more detached. In a side chapel
you feel close to human destiny,
can't turn eyes or mind from it.
The bareback rider on donkey
entering Jerusalem in the vault
of the west arm of the cross
of Peribleptos heads into a crowd
fixated on a liberator. Followers
press him forward. All eyes from
windows and street see a hero
on horse, not a man in common vesture
on an ass. All see what they want
to see and expect to be delivered
freedom on a bloodless platter.

Meteora

Monks and nuns in their eyrie
like transfigured eagles
with aureoles, angel wings,
eyes as accepting as setting
suns. True messengers of god
who never hunger for prey.

With minds sharp as talons,
fingers caress texts in glorious
libraries word by word while
on walls Lazarus rises in narthex,
haloed heads suspend above
bodies of disassembled martyrs.

Bells and chimes in courtyards
with manicured flower gardens
ring till the Last Judgment. At
reception a nun in holy habit
collects admission fees,
offers icons, booklets, CDs.

I leave with a remembrance
of Turks who first drove hermits
from the plain below. Overhead
fighter jets thunder like Zeus,
prepare to strike like Jehovah.
Saints in the chapel of Nikolaus weep.

Two Beasts of Burden

Donkey and laborer
wear down walkways
in the carless village
of Monemvasia —
one with hoofs,
the other with
bruised boots,
one backpacked
with cement,
the other gloved
with wheelbarrow,
one to clear rubble,
the other to build.
Both in measured
stride over steps
of unpredictable
height, length, depth
in defiance
of any scientific
theory of stability,
regularity, or chaos.

Flowering Rock

Iris, campanula, tassel
hyacinth blossom purple
in this land of rock
that shows no sign
it has time or interest
to nurture anything.
Wet with sea spray,
dry as a valley of death,
hard as granite, soft
as soapstone it struggles
just to resemble life.
Despite, and unaware
of its gift, it gives
mineral-rich footing
to wild flowers in stone
walls, fields of red
boulders, Achaean
acropoleis. Crevices like
micro-ravines too small
to be seen quench thirst,
feed roots with moist soil.

Rock unlike and like
the muddy birthplace
of the sacred lotus.

Fishing Early Spring

After a week of blows
from Aeolus and rough waters
from Poseidon, fishermen
shoot words at each other
like bullets, phrases from
automatic rifles. They'll
have two days to fill stainless
steel counters in shops, only
two days before April's full
moon drives fish too deep
beneath the illuminated sea.

Like hungry seagulls, three boats
in harbor pull up rusted machine
gears used for anchors. Two
others spot-scraped and freshly
painted leave a dead man's track
in sand when dragged past roots
and driftwood from beach to water.
On plastic take-away lunch plates
country bread and feta, onions,
tomatoes, lettuce tread olive oil
to keep from drowning.

Letter to Yannis Ritsos

—for Maria and Takis

"Rock. Nothing else," you once
called your birthplace and I
can number the reasons why.
A father who drank and gambled
family property away gone mad.
A mother who doted on your art,
poetry, curly blond hair, blue
eyes gone tubercular. A brother
lost to the same disease. A sister
to asylum. And your own tempestuous
shifts from spacious home to gate
house, stage to sanatorium, dancer
to guerilla, poet to prisoner,
dissident to exile. Such living
can make a rock of one's world.

I've woken to the pearl brilliance of the morning star
while those that sanctify your night fade,

watched rust work its devilry
on bands and locks of fortress doors,

– continued

tasted grains of salt on the cannon in the square,
on the bolts and keys of churches,

seen the winged lion above the bishop's doorway smile
when Turks surrendered town for crimson cloth and battle steeds,

smelled fish soup at Matoula's,
shared pomegranates with Persephone,

lamented the loss of your barber shop, shoemaker, fish market
to tourist cafes, souvenir and jewelry shops,

been scorched by your merciless sun,
washed by the cool hand of your sea,

labored with your dead step by uneven step on
carved rock from lower town to upper fortress,

climbed to the now chained door of Hagia Sophia
where Christ Pantocrator in fresco still survives,

imagined this fortress truly was Akra Minoa,
the true place of your birth.

I've not yet found your childhood
sling or the Argonaut's oar
among nettles, but have found
much more than rock here. I've
welcomed breezes on a burning
day, watched them pass through
open shutters to cool inhabited
insides, wend through window
frames of shattered corneas,
roofs with fractured skulls.
Next to your prickly pears
I've heard grape hyacinth
sing with drunken bumblebees.
I've seen your pin-striped
stars of white asphodel shine
on braided heads next to tall
yellow thorns and euphorbia
flow out of broken walls,
its flowers tiny lily pads
thriving in a land without ponds.

– continued

I admit to wearing corrective
lenses to protect myself
from your torturous trials
too painful for me to know.
And I shy from your flashes
of resurrection that struggle
to become one radiant blast
of light. I try to spread light
as your crown daisy does, its
heart of gold melted to lemon
for human eyes to adore.

I'm only a spring visitor to your
rock islet, never struggled so
through boyhood and manhood.
I'm simply one of those believers
that poems like yours cut from
jagged rock and shaped to finished
stone can make us more generous
than we think we can be. I stretch
my neck to see you drag your chains
past Elkomenos and to hear you
speak. You, like that other man
of passion, knew all thoughts
have been thought, all feelings
felt, and nothing ever lost. You
too made all times our eternal
moment. He a talker who could not
help himself from talking, you
a writer who piled words on words
on words till lain in familiar
soil under a grieving cypress.

Mediterranean Cypress

Kindly leave this umbrella
closed as it is. There's no
need to open it for brief
showers and it's not fancy
enough to spread its skeletal
ribs like a parasol to keep
the blistering sun off white
skin. Its bottom pole smooth,
its ferrule pointed. Leave it
a slender evergreen cone to mark
where solitary mountain chapels
in Lakonia are, or once were.
Or use it as you choose:
windbreak to protect sown fields,
tender crops; aesthetic pomp
by pillar or pool in your villa
garden; precious wood for Flamenco
guitars; memento mori in cemetery.
Its life spans centuries. Its sap
the tears of Kyparissos. Its dense
foliage shelter for song birds.
Strong, tall, upright, dignified.
Upside down it's an exclamation mark
for us to question death's finality.

Laundry Basket

Romani woven from weeping willows,
beige rods for pillars and plaited body,
auburn splashes for Jackson Pollack,
braid for handle, wreath for crown.

Stolen with impunity
from an olive grove in Crete,
this nomad transported to nestle in New
England grass beneath clean sheets.

Terraces

— for John

No row houses here,
just rows on rows
of hillside labored
by hand and shovel
rock by rock for sheep
to feed, olive trees
to fruit. A mirror
of terraced times
mythic and historic,
barbaric and heroic —
an archaic, classical,
Roman, Byzantine,
Venetian, Ottoman,
modern mix. Shelf-like
steps on steep slopes
to cultivate rotating
crops of culture.

SPAIN
Andalucía at War and Peace

Christian Light on Moorish Arch

I never thought a rainbow stained
until this glimpse in Mezquita,
the Mosque's heart defiled
by Spanish opulence, its body
shrouded in Baroque stone.

No longer can its Roman columns
planted with precise measuring rods
be a heavenly woodland open
to courtyard trees leafed emerald
and laden with orange suns.

Five Centuries

Matchbox hovels of splinters,
thinned garlic soup on table,
field rakes with rotten teeth rest
on walls. Stench of goats, donkeys,
oxen. Bodies pressed against
each other. Nowhere to hide.

A life to numb young men and old,
daughters and mothers. Cause welts,
leave scars, blister until heart
turns ruby hard and mind adamantine
for bloody reprisal hot, radiant,
furious as blue stars.

British Colonial Pluck

The plan hatched like an egg
with green rots and putrid smell
in no less a place than Simpson's
in the Strand. Chilled Evian
on the table, Laurent-Perrier, Brut
to come. RC editor Jerrold finishes
off six Loch Ryan native oysters,
Spanish press attaché Luis Bolin
his lobster soup. Before roast rib
of Scottish beef in its silver-domed
trolley for the Yorkshire man
and potted shrimps for the Malagan,
talk of a private plane for Franco's
return to Spain. The time ripe
as Wimbledon strawberries. Major
Pollard an easy tap for mercenary
chief, hard liquor and guns his coat
of arms. Former MI6 mate, Captain
Bebb, the pilot. At Simpson's: *Viva
la Monarquía!* Catholicism! Fascism!
For Bebb: "what a delightful idea,
what a great adventure." Three coups,
three years of war, half a million dead.

Remembrance

On one day — 6th of May, 1937 —
thirty-four villagers from
the small hill town of Casares
driven like goats or sheep
to the Estepona road for a White
Terror kill. Wives, mothers, sons,
daughters, husbands, fathers,
grandmothers, grandfathers.
The youngest Lucrecia Pozo Gil
18 years old, body slight as a pine
needle. The oldest Catalina Mena
Quiros, 70, body full as a melon.

On the memorial, torsos of a mother
or wife and old man sunk in stone.
Flesh of rough cast metal flows
like clay colored sea green
and ash. You hear the woman's
cries and the old man's silence.
Above them a muscular young man
bears a polished black tablet
with thirty-four names. Incised
at top: "Reprisals by the national
faction." At bottom in calligraphy
as if penned by a living hand:

– continued

"I am here to live
as long as the soul dreams for me
and I am here to die
when the hour arrives for me."

The site protected overhead
by red cork oak, silver olive,
carob with crescent seed pods.
Fresh bouquets lie where bodies
were thrown 20 feet below the road.

Thirty-four butterflies netted
and pinned under the merciless sun
by raging black bulls.

Two Sides

"... cruelty had entered into the lines..."
— Ernest Hemingway, *For Whom the Bell Tolls*

Ronda's forests hang like pelt on rock cliffs
unshakeable as judgments of the Inquisition Court
once housed in the Convent of Santa Domingo above,
its gorge deep as hatred in the Republican mob
that flailed and clubbed town Fascists senseless
before tossing their carcasses over its hairy sides.

Spanish Dawn

No tanks now in city squares
No rifles in the hands of boys
No smell of gunpowder on girls
No cartridge belts on men
No militia trousers on women
No blood lapped up by thirsty earth
No flesh or bone to feed it
No mounds of bodies to cover it.

Yet every morning the eastern
flank of La Herriza de Enmedio
appears black as a widow's dress,
its ridge humped like the back
of a dead soldier blanketed by a sky
steel gray as the bolt on a Mosin-
Nagant. The civil war forever to be
felt, never forgotten, unforgiveable.

Beach Walk

> "... the duende does not repeat himself,
> anymore than do the forms of the sea..."
> — Federico Garcia Lorca,
> *Deep Song and Other Prose*

Like blades of roadside grass,
the sea does not repeat itself.

Like fields on valley floors,
the sea does not repeat itself.

Like pastures on hillsides,
the sea does not repeat itself.

Like fractures in cliff faces,
the sea does not repeat itself.

Like mists in canyon clefts,
the sea does not repeat itself.

Like winds on mountain peaks,
the sea does not repeat itself.

Like clouds in bleached skies,
the sea does not repeat itself.

Like poems by Garcia Lorca,
the sea does not repeat itself.

Only the sun, the moon, and death
repeat themselves in Andalucía.

THE TASTE OF EARTH

Lorca's boyhood village flat
as Kansas plains, its main road wide
and dusty as if in a 50s Western.
His house washed white, door unadorned,
ground floor for living, top floor
for grain. Smell of animals, feed,
fouled straw in the courtyard.

In his father's fields he bends his
youthful back to match the laborers,
fingers earth like a plough, turns
up Roman shards, imagines Arabian
tiles, hears black poplars sing, dances
with gypsies. All root-bound to earth,
all fertile for poems honeycombed.

Cubist Portrait

Lorca on stage the flamboyant
performer, speech strong as deep
song, intellect electric, blood
on volcanic fire. Truth stalked
like a prize hound on scent,
beauty stalked like a mad lover.
Conviction hard as gypsy pride.
Charming well-bred schoolboy
playful as a clown. Tender as dreams,
troubling as nightmares. A Proteus
of light and dark freed from fitful
public selves only in his small
summer room at Huerta de San Vicente.
For rest, a simple single bed. For
fevered words in search of health
and clarity, a plain desk.

Deeper Than What Is

—for Luis

Lorca called his *Gypsy Ballads*
a retablo, a towering frame
of panels not on the altar.
His embroidered cloak of niches
filled with gypsies, archangels,
horses, rivers, Jewish and Roman
breezes. All visible but none cut
deep enough by chisel or knife
to resonant as glowing embers
or living blood of land. Rather
a book in which "hidden Andalucía
trembles," its pages to starve
hearts, feed souls, crush spirits
in order to raise them. Pain —
deep and black as jet — the only
figure for listeners to feel mortal,
breathe poisoned air and drink
spring water. Andalucía trembles
from poverty, servitude, persecution.
And Andalucía trembles with ecstasy
at the poet's loving speech
of anguish and compassion.

Lorca Returns to Granada

What if you had not left Madrid for your family home?

A bullet sharper than a peasant's scythe
would not have slit the throat of your songs.

Federico Garcia Lorca near Alfacar

It matters for a time
if a man dies. But no
matter, after all, why
or how or where his body
lies. No matter, after all,
a family feud or friend's
betrayal. No matter
two bullets in his ass
for being queer or one
in his head for politics.
No matter tossed in a ditch
near a single olive tree
or dumped in a mass grave
with the teacher and two
bullfighters who marched
with him from summer-camp
holding center to killing
grounds. In the park today
his plaque unreadable, pieces
of his poems tiled in bright
colors on a mortared wall
as if epitaphs on a headstone.
His body stilled somewhere
in the company of tens
of thousands. For the sake
of peace, not one called saint
or martyr. No need for relics.

A Vision

> *"Since childhood a grim vision of
> the peasant has stuck in my
> consciousness. I've seen him walk
> his hunger through village streets."*
> — Blas Infante

Dear father, dear mother,
what is that corky trunk
with gnarled limbs laboring
through our white village?

I see hunger beneath its bark,
feel despair in its roots.

Casa de la Alegría

Exterior stone coarse as peasant
cloth relieved by touches
of Moorish windows, Christian
arches. Interior rooms dark
as caves where tile walls glow
under half-light, shimmer
and flash in a kaleidoscope
of universal colors when Blas
Infante's pen glides over paper
or when he plays on black and
white piano keys harmonies of Jew
with Moor, Moor with Christian,
Christian with Pagan, Pagan with Jew.

Arroyo Hondo

In Casares, the hill village
of his birth, Blas Infante
saw his people like crag
martins twist and turn
with chirps through plazas,
streets, shops, watched
them settle into sugar cube
nests precariously perched
in its cliff face. And he
dreamed of them as eagles
strong-beaked, taloned, free.

I see here only the powerful
bodies of Griffon vultures
driven by bloodlust drift
and glide in wind currents
that control their every
move. They rise late morning
from distant mountain peaks
to hiss and grunt over decaying
flesh. Like the *falange*. Such
is life in this gorged valley
with its deep, profound stream.

Off the Seville-Carmona Road

No fear the headlights
from that '36 sedan would blind
deer, freeze them before the hit.
Its two unblinking eyes trained
on the back of Blas Infante
for a single, clean pistol shot.

After the brief echo, night
dawned black, Andalucía bled out,
its flag of green and white
furled, its anthem silenced.
In the road, white shirt red, suit
sullied, spectacles splintered.

Today graffiti on a shaded stone wall sings
Viva Andalucía Libre!

Hidden Remembrance

Same sculpture, same figures
sunk in stony anguish, same
polished black tablet held by
the cramped hand of the muscular
young man. This time February
17th, 1937, with names of nine
men aged 26 to 52 plus Diego Ruiz
Ocana shot Christmas Eve 1936.
This time open to valley below
and sky above, but closed to view
unless you walk the narrow track
around a half-built cemetery
to the backside of its hill.
Villagers would not have heard
the scrape of boots on rock,
slung rifles rub against brush.
At most, muted gunshots. Stones
the size of hearts have been placed
on the pedestal and 20 feet below
to circle the shared grave where
bodies lie beneath common nosegays.

Passage

In the mountain village
of Benadalid
coffined bodies stacked
in white niches rented
for a space in time
rest in comfort atop
the ruins of a Moorish
fortress until buried
in common ground
for eternity.

Don Quixote Tilts at Wind Turbines

— for Vicki

Used to plains, not ridges,
Rocinante labors up Manilva
hill, her master to slay
thirty or forty monstrous
giants whose blades turn
like windmill sails,
whose towers of white steel
are nothing like wooden
bodies. In God's service
to rid earth of vileness
the Don charges, head spinning
like an egg beater, heart
pounding like hoof beats
for Dulcinea, lance in hand
tight as a generator bolt
to nut, buckler flapping
like a grain sack on clothes
line against raging winds.
Rocinante hits fifth gear,
lance waves at the far distant
blade it passes under, buckler
flies like a frisbee, horse
and rider hit the turbine's

millstone-hard concrete base
and tumble through briars
down the hill. Sancho arrives
as fast as his ass can go.
Rocinante survives a bruised
shoulder. Her Don revives
with otherworldly gusto
fueled by renewable energy.

Torre de la Sal

"What will you do
after retirement?"
the sea asks the tower.
"Your outsides will be
scarred with graffiti,
your insides hollowed.
You'll be emptied
of pistols, rifles,
and sinister capes,
skulls cast in lead
and patent leather
souls. Helicopters
will no longer rattle
your stones, Nissan
vans no longer foul
your grounds." "I'm
planning," answered
the tower, "a fish
business, salt rather
than bullets, smell
of cod rather than
black powder. A salt
flat where you now
see only sand will
preserve me. My gift
to you will be peace
free of my vigilant gaze."

Cork Oak

— for Kelly

Unlike snake skin
shed without help
when the old suit
becomes too tight,
bark of cork oak
needs two strippers —
one with axe to cut
necklace and rulers,
one with hands caring
as an archivist
in white gloves
to peel away plank
the size of doors
thick as Persian
rugs. No harm,
we're told, new
skin grows as fast
as newborn cranes
sheltered in its
forests. 200,000
tons a year for
cricket balls and

shuttlecocks,
fishing floats
and wine stoppers.
An "extraordinarily
sustainable" crop
for irrepressible
pleasures.

Speechless below Benarraba

The old man poked
his walking stick
in the brush
on both sides
of the path
as if looking for
a lost gold watch.
He somehow knew
I would not understand
so when he found
an asparagus shoot
his smile sang
and his eyes danced
as he offered me
with the thrill
of castanets
a touch
of his treasure.

February in Casares

— for Nicole

The walk so steep
from village plaza
to car park, a young
wife big with child
catches up to me.
We share a bench

and she shares what
I cannot see: grape
vines with micro nubs
of green, rose buds
with unborn petals
nowhere to be seen.

Acacia pom poms
blaze yellow overhead
to welcome spring,
almond blossoms nudge
enwombed leaves
anxious to unfold.

No "Thou Shalt Not" in the Valley of Manilva

Yellow gorse on hills,
children splash in Caesar's bath,
crown daisies in fields.

Garden Potpourri at Casa Ceramica

— for Shirley

Ribbons and spikes of green,
ivy and straight-backed rosemary.

Cypress spears, lemon umbrellas,
pine pyramids, unruly figs.

Palm fronds thin as montures of fans,
loquat leaves thick as leather.

Glazed leaf of camellia,
dull leaf of dried bay.

Crescents of carob pods,
beads of black olives.

Shafts of sun on almond blossoms,
pools of shade beneath agave.

Steps uneven as furrowed clods,
paths flow like sea swells.

Grunts from colossal vultures,
madrigals from tiny blackcaps.

A garden free of bias,
open to all, sweet as mango.

Acknowledgments

Grateful acknowledgment is made to the publishers and editors of the following books and journal where several poems in this collection first appeared, sometimes in early versions:

Approaching Winter Solstice (Cobtree Press, 2003)

Bittern Sweet (Cobtree Press, 2007)

Building Relationships: Selected Works of Jim McCord and Bruce McColl (Green Lotus Press, 2010)

Yorkshire Dales Review (2010)

BIOGRAPHIES

Jim McCord is an emeritus professor of English literature whose poems have appeared in a variety of journals and three books.

Carol McCord is a lifelong hiker and former yoga instructor. Her photographs have been selected for exhibitions and publications in the United States and abroad.

SHANTI ARTS
nature · art · spirit

Please visit us on online

to browse our entire book catalog,

including additional poetry collections and fiction,

books on travel, nature, healing, art,

photography, and more.

shantiarts.com

www.ingramcontent.com/pod-product-compliance
Lightning Source LLC
Chambersburg PA
CBHW040624240426
43666CB00020BA/2911